PYTHON PASSION'S
Ball Python
ENCYCLOPEDIA

Pamela Trentham

© 2011 - 2015 by Pamela Trentham. The book author retains sole copyright to his or her contributions to this book.
Photographs by Pamela Trentham © 2015, except where noted. Photographs by Sandy McCoy © 2011, and photograph by Steve Beamer © 2015, used with permission.

All rights reserved. No part of this book may be reproduced in any form, by photography, photocopying, or any other means, or incorporated into any information retrieval system, electronic or mechanical, without written permission of the copyright owner.

All inquiries should be addressed to:
Python Passion Captive Bred Ball Pythons
Pamela Trentham
2421 Jericho Road
Maryville, Tennessee 37803
www.pythonpassion.com
pythonpassion@live.com

Table of Contents

Introduction 1
Anatomy 3
Selecting a Ball Python 9
Housing 10
Heating Methods 12
Lighting 13
Humidity 13
Substrate 14
Hide Boxes 14
Tank Furniture 15
Water 16
Feeding 16
Type of Prey 18
Food Refusal 19
Shedding 22
Quarantine 24
Ailments 24
Breeding Introduction 28
Determining Sex via Cloacal Probing 29
Mating 30
Building Follicles 33
Pre-Ovulation Shed and Glowing 34
Ovulation 34
Post-Ovulation and Pre-Lay Sheds 35
Nesting 36
Egg Deposition 36
Eggs 37
Incubation 38
    Artificial *39*
    Maternal *43*
Sexing Babies via Cloacal Popping 46
Neonates 48

Feeding Tricks for Picky Eaters 48
Assist-Feeding 49
Force-Feeding 50
Selling Babies 51
Genealogy 52
    Recessive traits 54
    Incomplete dominant traits 55
    Dominant traits 57
Closing 60

Foreword

First and foremost, let me tell you what this book is **not**: a morph guide. There are far too many morphs to list, there are new morphs found consistently, as well as endless possibilities of combination morphs. If this book were a morph guide, it would be out of date within one year's time. What this book **is**: it is both a husbandry and breeding guide as well as an informative text about the inner workings of the ball python, including mating and information on the development of the babies from pre-conception to hatching. This encyclopedia has been compiled by myself as a means to help educate the general public about the behaviors of ball pythons. Most of the scientific information provided here is drawn from Chris Mattison's *The New Encyclopedia of Snakes*, and you will find his book listed in the bibliography. However, the husbandry and breeding is drawn upon my personal experience from keeping and breeding ball pythons since 2000, as well as what I've learned chatting with other ball python enthusiasts. By no means is anything here set in stone; every amateur keeper has their preferred methods that work for them.

I would like to take this time to thank Sandy McCoy for her insightfulness as to maternally incubating ball python eggs in captivity. Without her careful observations and notes on the topic, I feel as though this book would not be complete. She has broken the topic wide open when many looked upon maternal incubation as merely luck, and has provided valuable information most keepers are not willing to try to collect.

Please be sure you are well-educated on the husbandry aspects of keeping ball pythons before you begin breeding them; your experience and understanding of their needs will greatly assist your breeding efforts, and you may very well need to draw upon that when rearing hatchlings. If one finds themselves not comprehending the breeding section of this book, it is best to take a step back and learn the husbandry first before proceeding with breeding.

Happy ball python keeping and breeding!
Pamela Trentham

Python Passion's Ball Python Encyclopedia

Introduction

A ball python's scientific name, *python regius*, means "royal python" and in Europe this is how they refer to them. Ball pythons get their nickname from their defensive habits; they roll into a ball when they feel threatened, drawing their heads deep within their coils in order to protect it. The reason they ball up is not completely known, but it is suspected that it makes them appear too large to be consumed by the black spitting cobras *(Naja nigricollis)* that prey upon them in the wild. Ball pythons have also built a slight resistance to black spitting cobra venom.

Ball Python Classification
Kingdom: Animalia
Phylum: Chordata
Subphylum: Vertebrata
Class: Reptilia
Order: Squamata
Suborder: Serpentes
Family: Pythonidae
Genus: Python
Species: Regius

Ball pythons are one of the smallest species of pythons, and their natural habitat, comprised mainly of grasslands, savannas, and sparsely wooded areas, is found throughout central and western-central Africa. They can reach a length of 4-5 feet, with females being the larger and heavier of the sexes. This species is mainly terrestrial (ground-dwelling), though on seldom occasions, they have been found in trees as high as four feet off the ground. These snakes are mostly nocturnal (active at night); wild populations of ball pythons spend most of their daylight hours hiding in termite mounds to escape the heat of the sun, emerging at night to search for food, mate, or carry on other day-to-day activities. They have a broad head covered by many small scales, and a rounded snout with visible heat pits along the labial scales. The head is usually black or brown and relatively unmarked, with the exception of a gold or tan stripe that runs from the tip of the nose through the eye to

Python Passion's Ball Python Encyclopedia

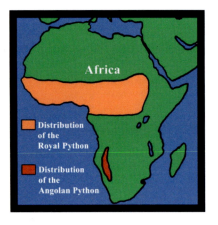

the back of the skull on either side of the head; this stripe helps to disguise the eye and break up the outline of the head. Their bodies are short and stocky, and are marked by a black background with gold to tan saddles. No two patterns are exactly alike, nor are the colors of each individual perfect matches to other wild type ball pythons. There are many variants in the saddle color, resulting in lighter individuals, average individuals, and darker individuals. There are also faded areas in the black coloring that many refer to as "blushing" that generally appear to be reddish or pinkish in young snakes and typically change to white or gray as the snake ages. Their closest relative is the Angolan python, which can be found in the wild in southwestern Africa; Angolan pythons look similar to the ball python, sharing the facial stripes, but the Angolan python is much darker and looks remarkably like a photographic negative of the ball python.

Snakes are ectothermic (also referred to as "cold-blooded"), meaning they cannot produce their own body heat; they must instead absorb heat from their surroundings. This is also the reason that snakes feed less often than mammals—most endothermic (warm-blooded) life must consume large quantities of food in order to produce body heat. Being ectothermic does have its advantages: this means that they can survive in areas where food is scarce; however, it also has its disadvantages as well: if the weather is cool, the snake is limited as to the activities it can perform as well as the time frame in which it can perform them. Ancient Romans believed that the ectothermic snakes had the power to take away fevers or other ailments, and therefore the sick would sleep in the temple of the god Aesculapius and allow snakes to crawl over them. Aesculapius carried a staff in the shape of a snake; the medical symbol today uses two intertwined snakes, deriving from this god.

Python Passion's Ball Python Encyclopedia

Ball pythons have a lifespan of approximately twenty-five years, though the record in captivity is forty-seven years; obviously, a pet ball python can live for quite a while, so one should be prepared to care for them for many years. It should be kept in mind that while many people keep snakes as pets, snakes of any species are by no means domesticated, and their natural instincts play the greatest role in their behavior, even in captivity. For example, snakes do not necessarily feel emotion towards their keeper; they may learn to recognize the certain scent their keeper has, or perhaps the vibrations made by their voice, and may even learn after prolonged periods that this particular person or persons will not harm them, but any resemblance to bonding ends there. Additionally, an enclosure should replicate the wild, even if it does not match exactly; instead of a termite mound for hiding, a ball python should be provided with some type of secure covering in which to hide. Without the ability to behave normally, captive ball pythons could be severely stressed, resulting in poor health.

Anatomy
Eyes: the ball python's eyes contain vertical pupils that are typical of nocturnal snakes which hunt at night, but they are poorly developed, and their vision is not great. Since snakes do not have eyelids, the eyes are covered by a brille, a special, clear scale that is shed periodically with the rest of the skin.

Heat-sensitive Pits: though not as advanced as the pits in pit vipers, these pits are similar, very numerous, and found along the labial scales, or "upper lips" of the python; they compensate for the poor eyesight by allowing the snake to "see" in

infrared when hunting prey.

Tongue: this is a forked appendage that is able to exit the mouth even while the mouth is closed through a notch in the upper jaw referred to as the lingual fossa. This allows the snake to "smell" the air without opening its mouth and causing movement, which could alert prey to its whereabouts. The snake extends the tongue and picks up scent molecules. The tongue is then drawn back into the mouth and inserted into the Jacobson's Organ.

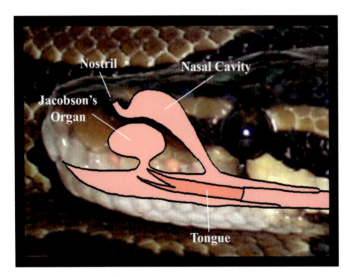

Jacobson's Organ: this organ is located in roof of mouth and connected directly to the olfactory lobe of the brain by nerves; it consists of a patch of sensory cells that detects moisture-bourne odor particles, while the nasal cavities detect airborne odors. This structure is especially helpful when hunting for prey or for mating.

Hearing: though snakes do not have external ears, they do retain the stapes bone, a small bone that makes contact with the quadrate bone. The quadrate bone is communicative with the lower jawbone, which is usually within close proximity to the ground. The vibrations felt through the lower jaw are in turn transmitted to the quadrate bone and then the stapes. Since snakes cannot hear in the same way as most animals, vocal communication has never formed between individuals. In turn, hissing developed as a defensive strategy rather than as a means of communication between individuals.

Python Passion's Ball Python Encyclopedia

Jaw structure: the common myth that snakes "unhinge their jaws" is completely false; the skull of a ball python has a lower (mandible) jaw in which the bones do not connect in the front center. The two ends are attached to one another by ligaments, and are capable of independent movement. The absence of a fixed lower jaw and the incredible elasticity of the skin around the jaws is what allows these independent lower jaw bones to spread open wide to allow for large prey consumption.

Teeth: ball pythons have four rows of teeth along the top of the mouth; two along the maxilla (outer edges), and two running down the center of the mouth, attached to what is called the pterygoid bone. They also have teeth along the ridge of the mandibles. All of the teeth curve towards the rear of the mouth, and are not present for the purpose of chewing, but for the purpose of capturing and swallowing prey; they aid in pulling prey down into the esophagus, where the swallowing muscles engage and assist in pulling the prey down the throat to the stomach. Snakes' teeth are continuously replaced throughout the animal's life.

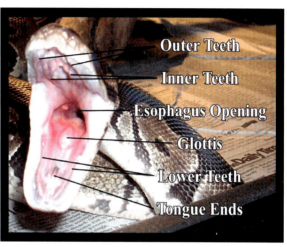

A large spur on a male ball python

Skeleton: this consists primarily of the skull and

ribs; the ribs are connected at the ends by muscles, which aids in constriction of prey as well as movement. Additionally, they have vertebrae in the neck (precaudal) and tail (caudal) that do not have ribs. They have no pectoral girdles (shoulders), but ball pythons do have a vestigial pelvis (hips), to which the spurs are attached; the spurs are used by the males during courtship and mating. Spurs are found on both males and females however, and should not be used to accurately determine the sex of the snake.

Heart: this is a three-chambered structure, comprised of two atria and one ventricle, in which the left and right atria receive blood from the body and lungs, while the ventricle allows blood to be circulated back to the body. The heart still functions very similar to the four-chambered mammalian heart, due to the divisions and valves within the ventricle. Since snakes lack a diaphragm, the heart is able to move about slightly within the body; this actually helps to protect the heart when large prey is being consumed. In opposition to amphibians, which rely largely on gaseous exchange across the surface of their skin, the snakes' pulmonary area of the heart does this for them.

Liver: the liver produces the bile that aids in digestion, and also excretes nitrogenous wastes and stores nutrients.

Spleen: the spleen works in conjunction with the gallbladder and pancreas to filter the blood and return the recycled blood cells to the bloodstream. The spleen also helps in producing blood cells in young animals, and in adults it aids in blood storage.

Pancreas: as in many animals, the pancreas produces and secretes digestive enzymes into the small intestine and controls the blood-glucose levels.

Gallbladder: this organ stores the bile produced by the liver and excretes these digestive enzymes to the small intestine when needed.

Lungs: while the left lung is considerably shortened due to the reptile's

Python Passion's Ball Python Encyclopedia

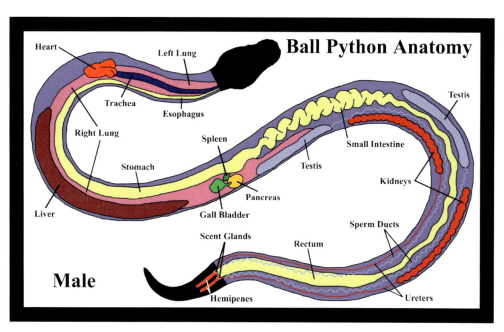

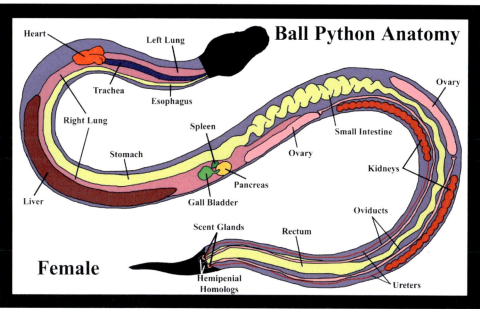

shape, the right lung is elongated to compensate; otherwise, snakes' lungs function and they breathe like mammals. However, oxygen exchange takes place in the portion of the lung closest to the head, while the lower portion is used as an air sac; the snake's lungs are not as well ventilated, and the excess carbon dioxide, the main waste of respiration, combines with water in the bloodstream to form carbonic acid, which breaks down to bicarbonate ions. Snakes have adapted to live to with higher concentrations of bicarbonate ions in their blood.

Trachea and Esophagus: the trachea is the tube leading the to lungs and is separate from the esophagus, the tube leading to the stomach, so that the snake may breathe while consuming large prey. The opening of the trachea, called the glottis, is very muscular, and can be pushed out of the mouth and held open in order to breathe while large prey is being consumed. The glottis has a vertical opening surrounded by cartilage and remains closed until the snake needs to breathe; when air is passed quickly through the glottis, it creates the hissing sound associated with snakes.

Stomach: the stomach begins where the trachea empties, typically about ¾ of the way down the liver, and is relatively simple, consisting largely of longitudinal folds that allow for flexibility and a large surface area in which to digest meals. The stomach ends at the pylorus, a tight valve marking the beginning of the small intestine.

Small Intestine: the small intestine is slightly coiled, but not as much as the life forms with more conventional bodies; since snakes are meat-eaters, they do not require a long and complex digestive system, and have therefore not evolved to digest vegetables or plants.

Kidneys: the kidneys filter the blood in snakes just as they do in mammals, though a snake's body is designed to eliminate waste with minimal moisture loss; therefore, snakes typically excrete uric acid, a white semi-solid, paste-like waste rather than liquid urine, and contains only enough moisture to allow it to move out of the body. The kidneys empty into the ureters; since snakes do not have a bladder, the widened ends of the ureters serve to store urine until it is expelled with the rest of the snake's wastes.

Male-Specific
- Testes: this is the organ that produces sperm.
- Sperm ducts: also called the seminiferous tubules, these structures are coiled tubes leading from the testes that carries the sperm to the bladder-like structure formed at the end of the ureters.
- Hemipenes: this is the paired male copulatory organ, and is located in the base of the tail and extends from the cloaca towards the tail tip. The surface of the hemipenes are covered with projections; these projections are thought to fix the hemipenes in place once copulation has begun. The hemipenial retractor muscles are attached to subcaudal vertebrae, and these muscles evert and withdraw the hemipenes.

Female-Specific
- Ovaries: this is the organ that produces and stores the eggs until they are matured.
- Oviducts: these tube-like structures store the matured eggs from the ovaries once ovulation has taken place; any stored sperm the female has retained, when released, fertilizes the eggs in the oviducts.
- Sperm Receptacle: this is the area where sperm from a male is stored until ovulation.
- Shell-Production Gland: this specialized gland is located at the posterior end of the female's oviduct, and it produces the eggshell just prior to egg deposition.
- Hemipenial homologs: females house funnel-shaped structures called the hemipenial homologs, and they are located in the same area the hemipenes would have formed had the snake been male, though they are much shorter than the actual hemipenes. They end in ligaments connected to subcaudal vertebrae in the tail, similar to the hemipenial retractor muscles in males.

Selecting a Ball Python
Ball pythons are one of the most docile species of pythons, though there

are exceptions to every rule, and one might on occasion run across an aggressive specimen; however, their mellow nature, relatively small and easily manageable size, and morphology has made them one of the most popular pets in the trade. When searching for an ideal pet, one should be looking for a snake that is alert, calm, has clear eyes, and does not have large folds of loosely hanging skin or a pronounced backbone. Also check to see if the snake has ticks, mites, scale rot, or burns.

Wild Caught (WC) ball pythons are those animals that were captured from the wild and exported for sale in the pet trade; Captive Hatched (CH) ball pythons are snakes whose mother was captured while gravid (pregnant), and was retained until she laid the eggs, which were incubated at a facility before being exported; Captive Bred (CB) ball pythons are those in which the parents were mated under captive conditions and the eggs produced from the pairing were incubated either maternally or artificially by the breeder after laying. Wild caught ball pythons often find it difficult to adjust to living in captivity, and are often riddled with parasites. Captive hatched babies tend to fare much better in captivity though they too may contain parasites, while captive bred babies are generally much healthier and free of parasites. Purchasing captive bred ball pythons support the captive breeders and reduce the numbers of animals exported from wild populations.

Housing
Since ball pythons are not social animals, they should not be housed with other snakes. In the wild, snakes are often found together, but this is usually a case of finding a suitable temperature in which to rest, not because ball pythons seek out the company of other snakes. In the wild, should a snake prove themselves a nuisance to another snake, one snake may simply leave the area and find another suitable place to rest; this is not the case in captivity, and either

would be unable to escape from their tormentor. Often times, keepers have observed their snakes "cuddling" together when they are housed in one enclosure; the snakes are not in fact cuddling, but competing for the "best" spot in the tank. This can cause dominance issues which can adversely affect one or both of the snakes. In addition, snakes that are housed together are much more susceptible to diseases that a cagemate might contract; it is often difficult to determine and isolate the ill animal, and therefore the illness spreads throughout to all snakes in the enclosure. Furthermore, though it is rare, ball pythons have been known to be cannibalistic in captivity; if the two snakes are similar in size, this will effectively kill both animals. Also, when snakes are housed together, they must be separated when feeding, and feeding outside of the snake's usual enclosure is not recommended; this will be discussed in more depth in the "Feeding" section.

While many fish grow according to the size of living quarters, this is not the case with snakes, and they will literally bust out the sides of their enclosure if kept in a space that is too small. While it is important not to house them in enclosures that are too large, it is also essential to make sure they have adequate space in which to provide a temperature gradient. The cool end of the enclosure should be 75-80° Fahrenheit and the warm end of the tank should be 85-90° F with an ambient temperature of 80-85° F. A basking spot at 90° F should also be available. This temperature gradient is important, as the snake will have the opportunity to regulate its own body temperature, and choose the area where it is most comfortable. This ensures the snake is always at the proper temperature, because it will go where it needs to be to regulate its temperature. Slight decreases in temperature of approximately 5° F overnight will not adversely affect the snake.

The tank should be sized according to the size of the animal; younger ball pythons stress much more easily if they are maintained in a large enclosure. As a rule, the long side of the tank should be two-thirds the length of the snake itself, though a tank this small may be difficult to find when housing hatchlings. A twelve-quart plastic shoe box with air holes drilled along the sides for ventilation often works well for

hatchling ball pythons, and can be heated with an under tank heat source. A ten-gallon aquarium also works well as a hatchling-sized enclosure. A large adult will never need a tank larger than a forty-gallon aquarium. Height is of less importance since ball pythons are terrestrial, and can be as short as twelve inches high. All snakes are master escape artists, and any type of enclosure that is chosen should be secure.

Heating Methods

Proper heating of a snake's enclosure is a must. The best things to consider are heat lamps or an under tank heat source (UTH) such as a heat pad, heat panel, heat cable, or heat tape. If an under tank heat source is used, a thermostat with a probe is necessary. Since snakes can only tell the difference between cold and hot, not hot and too hot, the thermostat will regulate the temperature in case the heat source gets too warm for the python. Any combination of these may be used to achieve the proper temperatures. A thermometer should be placed centered on either the front or back wall of the enclosure, two to three inches off the cage floor; this is done to monitor temperatures where the snake will spend the largest part of its time. Another thermometer with a probe should be used to monitor the temperature of the basking spot. While many may choose them for basking spots, reptile hot rocks should be avoided at all costs, as these items often malfunction, making burns imminent.

Lethal minimum and lethal maximum temperatures should also be taken into consideration. A snake's lethal minimum, in which case it would freeze to death, is approximately 38° F, and its lethal maximum is approximately 113° F, in which case it would expire from heat exhaustion. Critical minimum and maximum, 48° F and 95° F respectively, are the temperatures in which snakes may lose the ability of locomotion, and therefore cannot move to a more suitable temperature. Preferred body temperatures are between 69° F and 90° F; obviously, the higher preferred temperature is closer to the critical and lethal maximum, so it is important to keep a close eye on the temperature inside the snake's environment to ascertain that it does not get too hot. Since ball pythons in particular prefer a basking spot of 90° F, the basking spot should be heavily monitored.

While it is most certainly recommended that a ball python be handled regularly so it remains calm around people, keep in mind that ball pythons do have certain temperature requirements in order to remain healthy. A comfortable room temperature for a human being is much too cool for a ball python to spend the bulk of its time; therefore, it should be allowed back into its enclosure for the largest part of each day. Since ball pythons are relatively hardy animals that do not require strict constant temperatures, being out for a few consecutive hours will not adversely affect them; however, a python should not be allowed to sleep in the bed with its owner overnight or be allowed to roam freely in the house for a couple of days as this means the snake will be out of its recommended temperature range for far too long.

Lighting
Ball pythons do not require UV light like some lizards do. Often, a fluorescent bulb will suffice for lighting, though many choose to use a heat bulb. This provides the python with lighting and warmth. Either choice is acceptable, as long as one has an alternate heat source with the fluorescents. Ball pythons need to have a light cycle since they are nocturnal. A recommended light cycle of twelve hours of light and twelve hours of dark simulates the days and nights near the equator where the ball python is found in the wild. Commercial lighting timers can be used to achieve this, or one may simply turn the lighting off and on manually.

Humidity
Ball pythons should be maintained with 50-60% humidity, though this should be increased during shedding to 70%. When using glass tanks and

screen lids to house a ball python, it is often difficult to maintain proper humidity. One simple solution to this is to cover three-quarters of the lid with aluminum foil, and secure it in place with aluminum tape, which is widely available at many home-improvement stores. A humidity gauge should be placed near the thermometer in approximately the center front or back of the cage, but two to three inches above the floor; this is done so that the ambient humidity where the snake will spend most of its time is being monitored. A humidity gauge placed on the warm end of the enclosure will often read much drier than the rest of the tank.

Substrate

Pine or cedar should never be used as a substrate for a ball python! These woods contain minute particles that can be inhaled by the snake and cause respiratory problems. Other substrates to avoid are corn cob, alfalfa pellets, sand, gravel, and bark. Newspaper, paper towels, or aspen are some of the most common substrates used for ball pythons. Newspaper is the cheapest, though it does not provide a realistic appearance. Newspaper and paper towels are, however, very easy to clean. Aspen may be used to achieve a more realistic and attractive display tank; however, aspen holds humidity in very well. This can be helpful if one lives in a dry or less humid area, but this can also adversely affect the snake if too much moisture is being retained. Aspen may be spot-cleaned weekly, and a complete substrate change be done once per month, but keep in mind that even though snakes are designed to conserve as much moisture as possible when eliminating waste, captive animals are generally provided access to water much more freely, and it is often surprising how much liquid urates a snake can expel. When using aspen, be sure to remove any wet substrate during spot cleanings.

Hide Boxes

Hide boxes are very important for ball pythons and can actually play a role in whether or not the snake will feed, in addition to the snake's overall health: stress can make the snake more susceptible to parasites and can suppress the immune system; secondary problems include nutritional deficiencies, inactivity, and weight loss, which will ultimately make them more susceptible to disease; with an already weakened immune system, disease for a stressed animal can be deadly. When a snake is stressed, they like to have somewhere they can go to feel secure, and hide boxes provide them with  that. The hide box should be just large enough for the snake to fit into. If a hide box is too large, the snake will not feel secure. A hide box should be placed on each end of the enclosure so that the snake does not have to choose between preferred body temperature and security. A cardboard box with a hole in one end works well as a hide box, and there are commercial hides available online or at local pet stores. Anything that is opaque (not see-through) and is not made of pine or cedar will work as long as it has a hole in one end and is the appropriate size. Many choose to make their own hides for their older and larger specimens by purchasing a small cat litter pan, turning it upside down, and cutting a hole or doorway into one end; this is often a cheaper alternative than commercial hides, and are just as effective, even if they are not as attractive.

Tank Furniture
Tank furniture is necessary in tanks with a lot of wide open space left over after the water bowl and hides are provided. Ball pythons do not like wide open spaces, so something should be used to break up the snake's line of vision. Logs or artificial plants are acceptable and are widely available online or at local pet stores. Make sure any logs are heavy and do not rock. If they do, the

snake can harm itself with them. One may place their chosen log on the floor and press down firmly to determine if the log is stable. A log or logs may also be permanently mounted into the enclosure, thus providing the snake with a stable environment.

Water

Snakes do not lap up water with their tongue when drinking, but rather inserts the nose into the water and pulls water into the esophagus, similar to drinking through a straw. A large, heavy bowl of water is recommended and should be kept in the cage at all times. It should be large enough for the snake to fit its entire body inside for soaking purposes. This is especially important during shedding, because it helps loosen the skin for easy removal. The bowl should be heavy enough so that the snake cannot tip it over, such as a ceramic or heavy glass bowl with a low center of gravity. If the water bowl is tipped over by the snake, it is important that the bedding be replaced immediately.

If a snake lies in a damp area for an extended period of time, it can cause stomach rot. Scales or eye caps that are "wrinkled" or puckered are often a sign of dehydration, and may be rectified by making sure the snake has a constant supply of fresh water and proper humidity. Fresh water should be provided at least every three days.

Feeding

Feeding a snake outside of the snake's usual enclosure is not necessary. The idea behind this is so the snake will not associate the cage opening with feeding; however, this does not occur unless this is the single reason for the cage opening. If a ball python is being properly cared for, the cage should be opened for many reasons, such as feeding, cleaning, changing water, or handling. If this is the case, the snake will naturally figure out that the cage opening does not signal food; it could mean anything from feeding to handling. Additionally, moving a ball

Python Passion's Ball Python Encyclopedia

python around during the feeding process could cause unnecessary stress to the animal. Snakes should not be handled for twenty-four hours after feeding to avoid stress while the snake is digesting its meal, as this could cause a regurgitation. Furthermore, the keeper is more at risk for being bitten by their pet snake when the snake has finished its meal and is being returned to its usual enclosure since the smell of prey is strongest at this time.

The best way to size the feeder animal is to wrap the thumb and first finger around the largest part of the snake's belly. The diameter of the largest part of the belly should be roughly the same as the diameter of the feeder's body. Many people recommend feeding freshly killed or frozen/thawed rats or mice. This is a good idea. Feeding live rats or mice to a captive snake can result in injury to the python by scratching or biting. Many keepers will resort to live prey only when they are having trouble getting their ball python to feed, as this species can be particularly finicky. When feeding, do not offer rats or mice by hand, as ball pythons are aggressive feeders and one risks being bitten. Instead, offer feeder animals with tongs or other such instruments. Do not be alarmed if the snake chooses to constrict a pre-killed rat or mouse; this is the snake's natural instinct. A young ball python should be fed once every 5-7 days, and adults fed every 7-10 days; however, one may find that feeding every 7 days makes it easier to keep track of which day is feeding day. Once the snake has constricted its prey, the snake will begin to "smell" the animal by flicking its tongue along the feeder; this has often

been construed that the snake was trying to find the head of the animal to begin the swallowing process. While this is indeed true, the snake is also examining the size of the feeder as well, to determine if the prey can be successfully swallowed.

In the wild, ball pythons feed largely on African giant pouched rats, sometimes referred to as Gambian pouched rats (*Cricetomys gambianus*). These rats are nocturnal like the ball python, and sometimes lives in forests and thickets, but most notably in termite mounds where ball pythons are frequently found. These rats can reach lengths of three feet, though half of this length is tail, and reach weights of ten to fifteen pounds. These differ from common Norway rats by the presence of pouches in the cheeks, similar to a hamster. In captivity, common mice or common Norway rats are quite acceptable substitutes, providing the nutrition required for a ball python.

For a number of years, there were many discussions about the most nutritional type of food for ball pythons. While some argued that adult mice were best for young snakes, others disagreed and insisted young rats were better prey items. In recent years, studies have found that young rats are indeed much healthier for the snake in terms of growth. An adult mouse the approximate size and weight of a young rat was found to have smaller bones and internal organs, and found to contain more fat and less protein, thus making the mouse less nutritional. Also, since ball pythons can be finicky feeders, starting a baby ball python on young rats whenever possible eliminates the chances of the snake refusing to switch from mice to rats as they grow larger in size and can accommodate larger meals. It is not to say that feeding mice to a young ball python will adversely affect them, but in terms of growth, they grow much faster when fed young rats. It can be difficult to find young rats in some locations as feeders, however, and mice are still considered an acceptable prey item.

Type of Prey
- Live: although snakes feed on live prey in the wild and do often become injured, this risk of injury is higher in captivity. Should the

snake refuse its prey, it has no means of escaping from the rodent, and if the rodent is not supplied with food, it may very well begin feasting on the python in order to survive. Live prey is not recommended for captive animals, but should it be necessary, it is imperative that live prey always be observed while it is in the enclosure with the snake, and removed if the snake has not consumed it within thirty to forty-five minutes, as most likely if the snake were hungry, it would have already constricted it.

- Freshly killed (F/K) or Pre-killed (P/K): freshly killed (or pre-killed) prey is often a great substitute for live prey, with no risk of injury to the snake. Additionally, this type of prey is often used as a stepping-stone tool when attempting to switch a live-feeding snake to frozen/thawed prey.
- Frozen/thawed (F/T): frozen/thawed prey can be of great benefit to both snake and keeper; frozen prey is more convenient for the keeper, and actually benefits the snake by freezing and killing any parasites that might be within the feeder's body. It is often argued that frozen feeders are not as nutritional as live or freshly killed prey, but there have been no studies to prove or disprove this. For example, freezing could diminish slightly the amount of vitamin D within a feeder animal; however, there have been no studies done to prove exactly how much vitamin D is required by a ball python and therefore the amount provided in a frozen prey item, even if slightly diminished, may still exceed the amount required. The longer an item is kept frozen, of course, the higher the risk of nutritional depletion, but even feeders kept frozen for up to one year are not considered to be nutritionally deficient. Many keepers and breeders have their captive snakes on frozen/thawed prey, and there is no proof that these animals are any less healthy than those fed on live or freshly killed prey; similarly, breeder snakes fed frozen/thawed animals are no less likely to produce healthy eggs.

Food Refusal

If a ball python is refusing food, there could be any number of reasons why. In order to determine the cause of the snake's food refusal, one should ask themselves a few questions:

Python Passion's Ball Python Encyclopedia

- *How long have I had this pet?* If it's been less than 2 weeks, it's quite possible the snake is still a bit stressed from the big move; give him/her a bit more time to settle into their new surroundings.
- *What type of prey did the previous owner feed this snake?* As noted previously, ball pythons can be particularly finicky eaters, and can often be stubborn as to what type of prey they prefer. If the previous owner fed mice and instead, rats are being offered, this could be the reason why the snake is refusing meals. Likewise, frozen/thawed feeder items do not have as strong of a "food smell" to the snake, so even if the previous owner fed freshly killed prey, and they are being offered frozen/thawed, the snake may not be recognizing the frozen/thawed item as food. The best thing one can do is to find out for sure what type of prey the snake has been feeding on in the past and attempt to feed the snake the same. However, if the previous owner has been feeding live, it is highly recommended that they are switched over to freshly killed or frozen/thawed prey at the first opportunity, while recognizing that until the snake settles into their new environment, switching them may not be an option.
- *How often am I trying to feed my snake?* If feeding is attempted more than once per week, the snake is being stressed out. Offering food to a ball python that is refusing it every day or every other day is actually doing more harm than good. Cut back to offering once per week. If the snake continues to refuse meals, try offering once every two weeks. Additionally, offering meals that are refused week after week often gets the snake into the habit of refusing meals.
- *Have I offered different colors of rodents?* As strange as this may seem, on occasion some ball pythons seem to prey imprint on a particular color of feeder. Some may prefer solid white feeders, while others may prefer solid brown or black feeders. Some may accept "hooded" rats (those with colored heads and shoulders, and often a colored stripe or spots down the back) or solid white rats, but not solid brown or black ones. Experiment with offering different colored feeders to see if the snake accepts one over the other.

Python Passion's Ball Python Encyclopedia

- *Is my snake going into a shed?* Some ball pythons will feed while in the shedding process, and some will not, especially if the eyes have a milky appearance. Remove the feeder item from the snake's enclosure and wait until the snake has shed its skin before offering food again.
- *Is my ball python close to 1,000 grams in weight?* If so, they are nearing sexual maturity, and it is often noted that they have hit the 1,000-gram "wall" and begin to refuse food.
- *Is my snake trying to brumate?* Brumation, the reptilian equivalent to mammalian hibernation, is the most common reason for snakes to go off feed. Many adult snakes refuse food annually. If it's near October (sometimes as early as August, but this doesn't occur too frequently), food refusal is not at all uncommon, and many sexually mature snakes will begin to brumate in preparation for breeding; most snakes reach sexual maturity within two to three years, and at approximately 800-1500 grams in weight (males at the lower end and females at the higher end), though that does vary from snake to snake, as all will grow at different rates depending on the size and type of feeder offered as well as the frequency. It is also not uncommon for them to go the entire winter without accepting a meal. Often, they will begin feeding again in March or April. If a snake is of sexual maturity and they are consistently refusing food week after week during the fall or winter, it is highly advisable for the keeper to cool the tank by 5° F; this is done so that the snake's metabolism slows down slightly and they do not lose as much weight since they are not consuming any meals with which to replenish it. Be sure to wait at least three weeks after the snake's last meal before cooling them however; cooling them too soon can cause their last meal to sour inside their stomach and cause a regurgitation.
- *Is the cage temperature at the proper setting?* If the snake is too cool, they will refuse food as they do not have enough heat to properly digest their meal. Make sure the ambient cage temperature is 85° Fahrenheit with a basking spot of 90°.
- *Am I housing two ball pythons together?* If so, one may not feed because it feels dominated by its cagemate. Purchase another enclosure and place one of the snakes in it.

Shedding

Snakes' scales are formed from thickened areas of the skin by keratin, the same substance that forms humans' fingernails and hair. Ball pythons hatch with every scale they will ever have (as does every known snake on the planet as of this publication); that is to say, they do not grow new scales, but the scales they have simply grow larger. Scales aid the snake in many ways; they protect the skin from damage, as well as help to preserve moisture within the snake's body. The ventral (belly) scales also aid in locomotion. The outer layer of skin, the epidermis, is subjected to much wear and tear, and is therefore sloughed periodically in order to provide fresh protection. Ancient Greeks and Romans believed the snake had immortal life due to the shedding of the skin, even though the Christian religion has viewed the snake as a symbol of Satan. Traditionally, snakes' skins, in addition to snakes' gallbladders, were also used by humans to ease the pains of childbirth.

Before shedding, snakes secrete an oily substance between their two layers of skin: the outer layer, which is the layer that is seen, and the inner layer that continually forms between sheds. This oily secretion causes the colors of the skin appear darker, and the snake will have a bluish cast to its skin as well. A few days later, the eyes will cloud over,

A pastel ball python during and after shed

giving them a milky appearance; though the snake's eyesight is already poor, it is especially reduced during this time, and the snake may be more easily startled or frightened. Once the snake is ready to shed, the eyes will clear and the snake will begin to shed its outer layer of scales. It will begin at the nose and then  proceed forward, slithering right out of its old skin like a sock being turned inside out. When shedding is complete, simply remove the shed skin from the tank. The former inner layer is now the outer layer, and a new inner layer begins to form. The snake also has brighter color after a shed, due to the fact that this new layer has not been subjected to wear.

Younger snakes generally shed every four to six weeks, while adults may have more time between sheds. Healthy animals will shed in one, two, or three large pieces. If the animal sheds in many small pieces, it is probably because the humidity of the cage needs to be increased. To increase humidity, spray the cage with water two to three times daily. Inspect the snake after the shed, especially if it has shed in many pieces, to be certain that all the old skin has been removed, in particular the eye caps and the tip of the tail. Infection can grow if any of the old skin stays in place after shedding, and one will have to remove this skin. To do this, wet a pillowcase with warm water, squeeze all excess water out, place the snake inside, tie it shut, and place it in an open plastic tub under the heat lamp or over the heat panel in the tank. Leave the snake inside for one and a half to two hours, checking on them every thirty minutes. When all of the leftover skin is gone, including the eye caps, the snake may be removed from the bag. If any skin still remains, fold the skin back parallel to the snake's body and gently pull it off.

Python Passion's Ball Python Encyclopedia

Quarantine

It is highly advised to quarantine any newly-arrived snakes before introducing them into an established collection, regardless of from whom they have been purchased. Mites may come in on a new arrival, and can quickly spread to every animal within one's collection if the new snake is not quarantined; some serious and fatal diseases, such as IBD (Inclusion Body Disease) can rapidly wipe out an entire collection of pythons or boas, and quarantining new animals greatly reduces this risk.

A 90-day quarantine period is recommended. Proper quarantine should begin with housing the snake in its own enclosure, in a room away from any other established animals. Some ailments, in particularly IBD, are thought to be transmittable by both the air as well as the keeper, and it is best to keep this in mind when caring for a new animal. This snake should always be serviced last when feeding, cleaning, etc. Hands should be thoroughly washed and sanitized after handling the new arrival, its food, or its cage furnishings; many keepers will go as far as to change their clothing after working with a snake in quarantine. Do not place any other animals within the cage with the new arrival (other than its prey), and do not use its cage furnishings in another animal's enclosure without thoroughly cleansing and sanitizing these items. Do not use a quarantined animal's enclosure for any other animal without thoroughly sanitizing the enclosure. Breeding an animal that is in quarantine is not at all advisable.

When the new arrival completes quarantine without any incidents, it may be moved into the same room with other established snakes and may be bred if desired. Should any incidents occur during quarantine, the 90-day period should begin again after the animal's health has been re-established.

Ailments

This text does not contain a formal section on diseases and problems of ball pythons, and for a very good reason: there is absolutely no substitute for proper veterinary care of captive reptiles. When in doubt of a reptile's health, that reptile needs to be taken in to a qualified veterinary office for proper diagnosis and treatment; some symptoms of common ailments will be discussed here so that one may know when a veterinarian is required, and what to do until the veterinarian can be seen. Often times, many pet snakes are medicated by their keeper, and the keeper may or may not be administering proper medication for any given ailment. Medication of snakes should not be administered except under the supervision of a qualified reptile veterinarian. Additionally, issues with a reptile's health are often the result of multiple overlaying factors, so it is imperative that all of the individual issues are treated in order to return the snake to a healthy state. A fresh stool sample, whenever available, is often advisable to bring to the veterinarian's office along with the reptile to be treated; many internal parasites can be detected with a stool sample, and a veterinarian will need to know what problems he or she is dealing with in order to properly diagnose and treat the animal.

In order to learn of qualified reptile veterinarians in one's area, it is advisable to seek out local reptile or herpetological societies, or even local online forums, as many have sections for recommendation of local vets. Finding a qualified veterinarian for a reptile can prove difficult at times, depending on location; many mammal vets will see reptiles, but those vets may or may not be qualified to diagnose and treat reptiles. Medications or procedures that work for mammal pets typically don't work the same way on reptiles, and results may vary, so it is extremely important to seek out a veterinarian that is qualified to care for reptiles. Often times, one of the best questions to ask your potential reptile veterinarian is: "Why does my ball python's cage temperature need to be elevated to its warmest range when it is ill?" A veterinarian who understands reptile health will know the answer: "In order to properly medicate a reptile, the reptile needs to be at its warmest range so all of the medication administered will be absorbed by the reptile, and we aren't left guessing how much medication was actually metabolized and how much simply passed through the reptile." Mammal vets never have to consider this factor, since cats and dogs are "warm-blooded" animals and will absorb medication regardless of the temperature in which they reside, but this is something that absolutely must be considered when dealing with a "cold-blooded" animal, whose metabolism is dependent upon outside heat sources. If your chosen veterinarian cannot satisfactorily answer this question promptly, choose another veterinarian.

Mites
Mites are small, black, brown, or red ectoparasites that feed on the blood of an animal. They come out at night to feed on the snake in the softer skin between the scales. They are most often best seen near the eye. If one determines that a captive snake has mites, the first thing to do is to quarantine it from any other reptiles. Use newspaper or plain white paper towels as substrate until the mites are eliminated, and remove all cage furnishings and place them in the freezer until the mites are eradicated.

Next, place an airborne insecticide such as a "no-pest strip" in an area of the tank where the snake cannot come into contact with it. It may be placed above the screen of screen-top cages, or a small screen cage built around the pest strip and placed within the tank. Approximately 2 inches of strip should be used per 10 gallons of tank area. After 3-4 days, remove the strip, but repeat with a fresh piece of pest strip in 9 days since the strips don't kill eggs.

An alternative to pest strips is using a mite spray for the animal(s); remove the water bowl and soak the animal in lukewarm water. Be sure to use a container with ventilation and a secure lid, and fill the container with enough water to submerge the snake halfway up the side of its body; water that is too deep can tire the snake out if they have to struggle to keep their head above the surface. Soak them for approximately 60 minutes, then remove the snake and towel dry the animal, finishing by spraying mite remover onto hands and rubbing the reptile down thoroughly until damp. The tank should be sprayed down heavily with insecticide, washed with a strong bleach solution, and then rinsed thoroughly with fresh water. Leave the water bowl out of the tank until the following morning so the reptile can't wash the spray off of itself. Allow the tank to air dry completely before adding fresh substrate and returning the snake to the enclosure. This process should be repeated once every three days until the mites are gone. It is advisable to treat one additional time after all mites appear to be eradicated.

Respiratory Infection (R.I.)
Raspy breathing and excess saliva are the most common signs of respiratory infection. Elevate the cage temperature to 88-95° F to assist in treating, and promptly call a veterinarian to make an appointment. R.I. requires proper veterinary care for successful treatment.

Infectious Stomatitis (Mouth Rot)
Mouth rot is characterized by cheesy-looking material along the gums of the snake, and in extreme cases may force the mouth open. This problem is usually caused by unsanitary cage conditions, rodent bites, stress, or any combination of these. Since this disease can cause permanent disfigurement if not caught and treated early, it is imperative that the mouth be treated immediately. Swab the outside of the mouth with cotton to remove foreign material, then treat the affected areas with hydrogen peroxide or unflavored Listerine (the affects on animals have not been tested with flavored Listerine, so only the original should be used) once per day, and may be required for up to 2 weeks. A veterinarian should also be consulted, and an additional antibiotic may be prescribed in order to fully correct the problem.

Thermal Burns
Thermal burns can be easily prevented. Make sure the snake's hot spot in the enclosure is not getting too warm; a thermostat with probe is the best way to combat this problem. However, should the snake receive a thermal burn, the burned area will appear to have a large, brownish blister filled with fluids. Treatment of thermal burns must be administered by a qualified veterinarian. The burned area must be scraped and rinsed with saline. The snake will also require soaking for 30 minutes each day, as well as additional saline rinses and application of silver sulfadiazine cream twice daily. The snake will most likely go

into a rapid shed cycle, though it may take a few sheds to see any improvement.

Breeding Introduction

Breeding ball pythons is usually very easy. Most ball pythons breed readily in captivity as long as they are healthy animals. Those kept at optimal conditions and that are fed properly will produce many clutches of eggs; in fact, it is thought that once ball pythons reach sexual maturity, they are able to reproduce until they die. Proper care and knowledge of the animal should be mastered before attempting to breed these animals, as the experience will assist in breeding efforts in addition to helping to produce healthy babies.

Male ball pythons can and will breed with a number of females in the same season if given the opportunity. However, the male's body weight and overall well-being should be considered during the breeding season. Males as small as 300 grams have mated successfully to produce viable eggs with the female; however, males should be at least 800 grams before any serious attempts to breed are made. During the breeding season, males will willingly go for months without food if they smell the pheromones of the female. This is not good for the male ball python, as he can lose far too much body weight and become very weak. During the breeding season, it is essential to keep a close eye on the male(s) and make the decision to pull them out of the mating processes if he exhibits signs of exhaustion. If this is the case, place him in a room away from all females in order for him to regain his desire to feed instead of breed.

Each female ball python can lay one clutch of eggs per year, provided that she has stored enough fat during the previous year. Only female ball pythons at least 1200 grams in weight should be considered for breeding, and 1500 grams is recommended. Bigger females mean bigger clutches of eggs or larger eggs, which transfers into healthier babies. The smaller females, however, are more at risk for stunting their growth should they be bred too early. The best thing to do is not get ahead of yourself—or your snake, as the case may be—and let her gain the proper weight before attempting to breed her. Feed her well while she is accepting meals, but do not power-feed. Just as breeding too young can cause problems, power-feeding can also cause problems, because while the snake's weight might be up to par, her reproductive organs probably are not. Also, females that are overweight typically either tend to lay infertile eggs, also called "slugs," or simply don't clutch at all. Feed them a regular schedule of one prey item every 7-10 days until they gain sufficient weight. Females usually stop feeding in November or December and do not begin feeding again until after the clutch is laid. It is possible, however, for the female to accept a few meals in the spring before she ovulates.

Determining Sex via Cloacal Probing

Obviously, one will need at least one male and one female in order to breed, but one must be certain they have obtained one of each sex. Cloacal probing, or more often referred to as simply "probing," is a method of sexing snakes that was first described in 1933 by Blanchard and Finster. Fitch detailed it in 1960, but most keepers did not use the technique until Josef Lazlo published two short papers in 1973 and 1977. Prior to this, most keepers had no way to accurately sex their

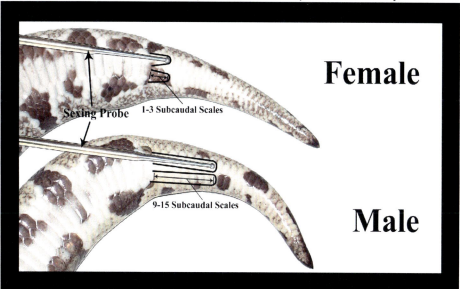

captive snakes. Probing involves the use of sexing probes, which are long, slender stainless steel probes with a ball on the tip; the ball tip helps to reduce injury to the snake being probed. The probe is first lubricated, then inserted into the cloaca of the snake to be sexed to determine if the probe can easily be inserted into the area where the hemipenes are located in males, which extends from the cloaca towards the tip of the tail. Females house hemipenial homologs, as described in the "Anatomy" section. Since hemipenial homologs are much shorter than the actual hemipenes, the probe will travel much farther in males, usually the length of 9-15 belly scales, as opposed to the 1-3 belly scales it will travel in females. Probing is not a surgical procedure; when inserting the probe into the snake, one is simply entering the inverted hemipenes (the exterior surface when the hemipenes are everted). Snakes are not easily harmed during this procedure, but one should still be gentle when inserting and pushing the probe.

When probing, be sure to use the largest possible probe to be comfortably inserted into the hemipenes should the snake be male. If smaller probes are used, it is quite possible to incorrectly sex the snake, since a small probe can pass relatively deeply into the females' hemipenial homologs and possibly tear the ligaments at the end or puncture the wall; should this occur, it will not affect the health of the snake, but this appears never to repair itself, and can make sexing the snake in the future difficult. Since this does often occur, it is best to probe both sides of the cloaca; the hemipenes of males will be almost identical in length, while females may probe to different lengths, especially in those with damaged hemipenial homologs.

Mating
Breeding season begins in the fall, and is stimulated by a shortened photoperiod and changes in baromic pressure; the latter seems to be the most prevalent stimuli, and many breeders have observed their snakes becoming more active at odd times, such moving around their enclosures during the day, once the pressure changes. Food refusal follows shortly, with males typically refusing food first in the early fall, followed by the females in late fall or early winter. Pairs should be

cycled together from October or November until the female ovulates or the male loses interest. Ovulation can vary from March to June, and though some females have ovulated as early as December or as late as October, this is uncommon. Since ball pythons typically ovulate in the spring so that egg-laying coincides with warmer temperatures for incubation, a female that has mated with a male in October most likely will not immediately ovulate and lay her eggs. She may mate several times with a male (or several males) throughout the course of the fall and winter breeding season before ovulating and laying eggs in the spring.

While many keepers never change their temperature or lighting cycles, some breeders have better success at doing so. If you plan to do so, at the beginning of October, change your light cycle to ten hours of daylight and fourteen hours of nighttime. Some choose to adjust more slowly, increasing nighttime duration for one hour for the first couple of weeks, then adding an additional hour of darkness. Either choice can work. Lower the ambient temperature by 5° F, but make sure your basking spot is still at 90° F, especially if you have snakes that are still feeding or are still expected to feed. Some breeders do not immediately cool their snakes at the beginning of the breeding season; waiting until December to lower the tank temperatures can on occasion work better, particularly if some are still consuming meals. Return temperatures and lighting cycle to normal in early to mid-March.

The male should be placed in the female's enclosure once breeding is ready to begin, since males tend to care less about their living quarters during the breeding season. Once a male is placed in the female's cage, some females, especially the younger ones, begin to scent their cage. Often times, the scent glands are erected, and the female begins to "wag" her tail while making laps around her cage. Urates and occasionally small traces of blood are expelled during this process, but this is nothing to be concerned about. Upon placement in the female's cage, the male typically begins stimulating the female by flicking his tongue along the female's sides and back. Eventually the male positions his tail near the female's and begins using his spurs to "tickle" the female into position for copulation. If the female is receptive, she will lift her tail slightly to expose her vent, and the male will coil his tail underneath hers and insert one of his hemipenes; males only use one hemipene at a time during copulation, though either  one may be used during any given breeding session. Hemipenes do not have a duct, but rather an external groove that, once inserted into the female's cloaca, forms a duct that allows the sperm to travel along. Females store sperm from males in the seminal receptacle; female ball pythons have been noted to store sperm for an entire year or more. Mating can last for as little as eight hours or as long as seventy-two hours. The pair should be left together until they separate, in which case the male should be moved back to his usual enclosure. In order not to wear the males out, any males that have bred should have at least 3-4 days in which to rest before he is placed with the female again, or with another female.

Should the male be unsuccessful in mating, a few tricks can be tried in order to attempt to stimulate the pair to breed; one may try lightly misting the pair with water, or placing the pair together when periodic low pressure is in effect, such as when a storm moves into the area. Provided both the male and female are healthy and properly fed, and it is the correct time of year, male-to-male combat generally isn't necessary, and the dominant male can cause serious injury to the submissive male in captivity since the submissive male cannot exit the cage. A much better idea than male-to-male combat is using a shed skin of another sexually mature male in the cage with the breeding pair; this stimulates the male to breed the female without the risk of injury. These tricks do not always work, but they can aid in assisting a reluctant pair on occasion. No tricks will work if either snake is unreceptive to breeding; this can mean the female is not yet ready to mate for the season, or that the male is not yet interested in mating. Continual introductions and separations of the pair typically yield results.

Building Follicles

The female will begin to build follicles typically in the late winter or early spring. The start of this procedure is not visible to the naked eye, but if the female has stored enough body fat, this fat will begin to form into yolk around the unfertilized eggs in the ovary; this process is called vitellogenesis, more often referred to as "building follicles." If the female has not stored enough body fat, the eggs will not mature, and will not develop further. Once the female begins building follicles, she will seek out the cooler end of the cage. Often times, she will be observed hugging the water bowl and "lumping up," a term used to describe the look of the females when they appear to have lumps or kinks in their body. Females often overproduce matured, yolked eggs, and any unused matured eggs are reabsorbed by female. There is speculation that the females use this to adjust the clutch size right up until ovulation. It is believed that snakes have the ability to determine how many eggs they will lay; they lay in larger numbers if food is abundant, and lay smaller numbers if food is scarce. In effect, there is a trade off between clutch size or hatchling size: the fewer the eggs, the larger the babies will be and subsequently they have a better chance at survival were they still

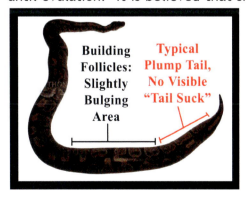

Building Follicles: Slightly Bulging Area

Typical Plump Tail, No Visible "Tail Suck"

in the wild since they are slightly less at risk for predation and may find food more easily due to the fact they can consume larger prey; the more eggs, the smaller the babies will be, but if food is abundant, the larger numbers of hatchlings should not have trouble finding adequate food. At around six weeks prior to ovulation, one can noticeably see the building; the female's belly will begin to swell slightly, and this is often mistaken for ovulation by novices. Ovulation is much larger, however, and it is very obvious once the females ovulates.

Pre-Ovulation Shed and Glowing
Shortly before ovulation, sometimes as early as six weeks, the female will shed, and they appear to have a "glow" to them. Their color brightens up drastically and very noticeably. A complete color change is absolutely amazing to see, and often keepers will wonder where the snake in their cage came from. Their color is so vibrant they almost look like a completely different snake, and they appear to have a high amount of blushing, which is extremely evident around the head and upper neck. Many breeders say their normal ball pythons almost appear to look like the ghost ball python morph when they are glowing; ghosts are known for their incredible blushing and reduced black pigmentation, which often occurs in glowing normals.

Ovulation
Eventually, the eggs completely mature and break through the wall of the ovary. They are caught by the oviduct via the infundibulum, the oviduct's funnel-shaped opening, which swells up around the ovaries at this time. Even though the infundibulum swells, some eggs are lost in the body cavity or caught by the oviduct on the opposite side. Once in the oviduct, eggs will be fertilized if viable sperm is present, either from a current mating session or from stored sperm, and will remain in the oviduct during development. If sperm is not viable or not present, the female will either reabsorb the eggs, or lay infertile eggs, called "slugs." If sperm is present, however, and the eggs are fertilized, they cannot be reabsorbed.

Externally, ovulation is visibly evident due to a large mid-body swelling.

Once the female has ovulated, it is easy for the keeper to see the difference in building follicles and ovulation; the female will appear to have swallowed an enormous meal. Ovulation is also accompanied by the "tail suck" in which it looks as though all of the fat has been sucked out of the tail. Once the female ovulates, she will then gravitate towards the warm end of the cage to further the

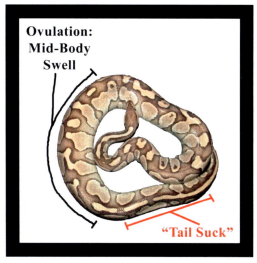

development of the eggs. Gestation usually takes from 50-70 days, and can depend greatly on the temperature; females kept at proper temperatures and that are allowed to bask often lay their eggs earlier,

while those kept at lower temperatures tend to hold their eggs longer. Most, but not all, female ball pythons will begin to lay inverted (with their belly in the air) sometime during egg development. It is not known precisely why the females do this, but there is speculation that this is more comfortable for the female, or that the eggs are getting better heat. Perhaps it is a combination of both.

Post-Ovulation and Pre-Lay Sheds

Approximately 15-20 days after ovulation, the female will shed; this shed is referred to as her "post-ovulation shed," and this is the best time to begin counting down until egg lay. Females typically deposit their eggs 25-45 days after they have shed. At this time, it is best to place a tray filled with barely damp sphagnum moss over the heat pad inside the tank with the female. If a female does not find a suitable place in which to deposit her eggs, she may either hold them or lay them in an inappropriate place such as the water bowl. If the eggs are to be artificially incubated, this is also the best time to set up the incubator; if using a hova bator, this is an especially good idea since hova bators' temperatures are known to fluctuate greatly for the first 2-3 days. Females that retain eggs longer may also shed a second time prior to egg lay; this shed is referred to as the "pre-egg-lay shed."

Nesting

Females look for the most suitable site for egg laying, though that can be minimal in captivity. They want a secure, covered area that reaches 89-90° F and has nearly 100% humidity. If provided with a nesting box, females will often move it around in the cage until it reaches the desired temperature; if this occurs, the keeper should not readjust the position of the nesting box. Humidity is difficult for the female to control herself in captivity, though during maternal incubation, females have been observed tightening and loosening her coils in order to allow more or less humidity to her clutch.

Egg Deposition

Ball pythons are oviparous (egg-layers) and the developing offspring are therefore enclosed within a parchment-like eggshell shortly before laying. A special gland in the lower part of the oviduct produces the shell. Sometimes two ova are enclosed within the same shell, resulting in "twins" in an egg, though all offspring birthed at approximately the same time by one mother in one clutch are technically considered twins, triplets,

quadruplets, etc. Most "twins" in eggs is probably a malfunction of shell production, though it is possible that some twins occur in the same manner as mammalian twins, with a single fertilized egg splitting into two separate embryos; this is suspected when observing two-headed snakes: these specimens may be examples of eggs which did not entirely split, or they may be visible evidence of chimera, which will be discussed later.

Females will usually get very restless just before laying their clutch. They may fold their body into odd positions, and crawl restlessly around the cage before settling down to get to work. Eventually, the female makes a nest for herself and begins the laying process, most often in the very early hours of the morning when it is quiet and very dark. They are often very nervous during this time, and any disturbance will agitate them, since they feel particularly vulnerable when clutching.

Eggs

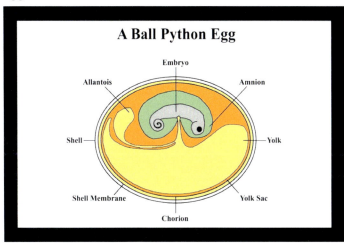

Ball pythons typically lay between 4-6 eggs, though there have been as many as 16 recorded in a single clutch; the younger the female is, the smaller her clutch will be. Each egg is made up of the shell, the shell membrane, the amnion, the chorion, the allantois, an albumiun, and an air bubble, in addition to the embryo and yolk. The developing baby is connected to the yolk by an umbilical cord. The albumin is composed of proteins and attracts water into the egg through osmosis; the air bubble acts as a pressure regulator and controls the exchange of oxygen and carbon dioxide. The shell and shell membrane are the only parts produced by the mother. The amnion, or the amniotic fluid; chorion, the sac surrounding the amniotic fluid, yolk, and embryo; and the allantois, which helps to regulate the exchange of gases as well as handles liquid waste from the embryo, are very thin membranes produced by the embryo. All of these membranes help to conserve water, which is the biggest difference between reptile and amphibian eggs, and the adaptation of this shelled egg have allowed reptiles to live completely independent of the water.

Incubation

Incubation will be broken down here by methods: artificial and maternal. There is much debate as to which method is best. Though artificial incubation seems to be the most widely used method, many have overlooked successful maternally incubated clutches, often writing them off as merely luck. Nevertheless, there are positives and negatives for either method, and the pros and cons should be weighed in order to make an informed decision. Studies have shown that maternally incubated eggs are less prone to desiccation as opposed to when artificially incubated; however, maintaining consistent temperature and humidity can prove difficult, especially for the inexperienced keeper or breeder, and particularly when maintained in a glass enclosure ventilated by a screen top and heated with lamps. Females will often begin feeding sooner and more consistently when the eggs are removed for artificial incubation, but many breeders who have successfully maternally incubated their eggs have provided data that falsifies claims that brooding mothers will not feed throughout incubation. However, not all females will feed while brooding, and those that do may typically feed on smaller meals less consistently, especially when in comparison of females whose eggs have been removed.

Whichever method is used, it is important for the breeder to be prepared to care for the eggs, whether it is through maternal assistance or complete care through artificial incubation. While the eggs are not particularly fragile and may withstand many changing conditions in the wild, it is important to understand the needs of the eggs, and this is much easier to accomplish with artificial incubation, and it is therefore highly advised that artificial incubation be mastered before maternal incubation is attempted.

Artificial
The first order of business when artificially incubating is to remove the mother from the eggs. This can prove problematic, since even the most docile females can become extremely aggressive when protecting a clutch of eggs. To remove the female, one should grasp her firmly on the lower neck and lift her slightly off of the pile; with the other hand, grasp the lower portion of her body and as gently as possible, unwrap her from the eggs. A thumb should be ran down her underside to determine if there are any more eggs left to be laid. If so, replace the female on her eggs and leave her alone. Check back in a few hours to determine if she has laid any remaining eggs.

Once the female has laid all of her eggs and she has been removed from the pile, the eggs may be candled for viability before placing them in the incubator. To determine if an egg is viable, use a strong flashlight (an LED is recommended) in a dark room, and hold the flashlight against the eggshell. If the egg is viable, one will observe a series of veins running through the egg.

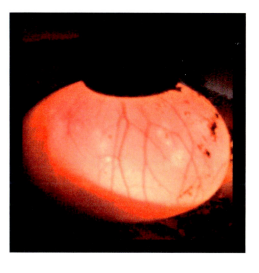

For the incubation medium, a mixture of vermiculite and perlite is recommended; the perlite added to the mixture allows for better air flow around the eggs. To mix this, add one cup of perlite to every two cups of vermiculite, then dampen it with water. Squeeze out all excess water, as the medium should be *damp*, not wet. The incubator should be filled with 5-6 inches of this mixture and a depression made in the

Python Passion's Ball Python Encyclopedia

center for the egg mass to rest. Place the viable eggs into the incubator, moving them with the same side up so as not to disrupt the air pocket inside at the top of the egg. Throw away any eggs that are not fertile. If eggs stick together, do not attempt to separate them; move them as a unit. If infertile eggs are among these, it is okay to leave them alone; they will not harm the other eggs. Once all of the eggs are in the incubator, surround them with the medium about ¾ of the way up. If using a hova bator, mostly burying the eggs with the medium is recommended; since hova bators are short, the heat source will be very close to the top of the pile, and can dry out any eggs there. Covering them with medium helps them to retain their moisture, and minimizes the risk of condensed water dripping down from the top of the incubator. Mostly burying the eggs can also aid those whose egg boxes are notorious for allowing water to drip down onto the eggs. While the eggs require moisture, direct contact with water will drown them.

Eggs swell in girth, especially during the first two weeks of incubation, due to moisture passing through the shell and being consumed by the embryo; if the medium is too dry, the developing baby will dehydrate and die, and the egg will soon begin to collapse. If the eggs begin dimpling, they are beginning to dehydrate. It is extremely important to note here that spraying the egg box or incubator will adversely affect the eggs, often killing them, and one should not attempt to increase humidity in this manner. Add moisture by pouring water in the medium around the eggs, but do not pour water directly on the eggs. Add water slowly, and check them each subsequent day to determine if they have regained their tight, inflated state. Once they become turgid to the touch, one has reached the desired moisture level. Incubation range is 89-90° F, though a degree on either side of the range does not appear to adversely affect the hatchlings, for a duration of 50-60 days. The lower end of the incubation range tends to produce hatchlings in the latter end of the range, while the higher temperatures of the incubation range yields hatchlings earlier in the range. Incubation temperature is also suspected to influence the babies' aggressiveness and even their feeding habits; higher temperatures may produce more aggressive yet better feeding hatchlings, though this has not yet been proven.

Throughout incubation, the incubator should be opened once every three days for approximately sixty seconds to allow for air exchange. The eggs will begin to deflate the last two or three weeks of incubation, and it is generally best to open the incubator more frequently during this time, typically once every other day, to allow more fresh oxygen to the eggs since this is the period in which the embryo draws calcium from the shell to form its bones; this allows for more oxygen into the egg as the shell is becoming weaker, and compensates for the added oxygen the embryo needs during this time. Eventually though, there is not enough oxygen for the fully formed baby, and it begins restlessly thrashing about within the egg; its egg tooth simultaneously slits the shell and the baby begins to hatch. Hatchling snakes will rest in the egg for up to forty-eight hours after making the first slit in the shell; it is important that the

babies remain in the egg during this period, as they are still absorbing the yolk and will not leave the egg until this process is complete. Once the baby fully emerges, it should be given its own enclosure containing a warmed hiding spot and access to water. If excess umbilical material is present, the baby should be  housed on damp paper towels until it disconnects; once it is removed, the substrate should be replaced with dry paper.

Egg-cutting is practiced by many keepers once the first hatchling pips in order to keep the neonates from "drowning" if they are not able to slit the egg on their own; however, egg-cutting is not necessary. Eggs hatch naturally in the wild without assistance, and are fully capable of doing so in captivity as well. However, should one decide to cut the eggs for any reason, such as a potential problem with an egg, one should pinch the top of the shell first in order to avoid snipping the membrane within, and make a small slit with a pair of scissors. It is important not to break the membrane surrounding the neonate; if this membrane is broken before the baby has developed the capability of breathing on its own, the baby will perish.

Most of the time, egg-cutting is done merely to satisfy the curiosity of the breeder and not for the sake of the hatchlings. However, it is possible to identify some morphs by candling the eggs at around day 40 of incubation. Some morphs are easier to make out than others, and this does not always work with multi-gene animals, but some basic single-gene animals can often be distinguished in this manner. Eggs containing albino or blue-eyed leucistic babies will have no discernable pattern within the egg, while normals produce strong dark pigments even through the eggshell. Some lighter-colored morphs such as pastels or butters and lessers can often be differentiated from normals as well when candling, due to the difference in intensity of the pigmented areas. Also, certain patterns like spider or pinstripe can often be seen. It is not a foolproof manner of determining which morph will come out of a particular egg, but it can help to satisfy the breeder's curiosity without potential harm to the developing babies, and it still leaves some room for excitement when the eggs do begin to pip.

Maternal
The most important elements to consider for maternal incubation are temperature and humidity. If a cage that promotes proper health is consistently maintained, such as those in which intact sheds are produced, success of maternal incubation is much higher. Humid hide boxes may be required in cages that are ventilated with screen tops and heated with lamps, however stackable cages or tubs tend to hold in better humidity and therefore a humid nesting box may not be essential. When humid hides are necessary, it is important to provide any females expected to maternally incubate their clutch with the nest box well before their egg deposition date so that they may familiarize themselves with the new addition in their enclosure and become comfortable enough with it to use it for nesting.

Photo courtesy of Sandy McCoy

When artificially incubating, the keeper must control all aspects of temperature and humidity, but when maternally incubating, the female is in control of this and the keeper has less hands-on responsibilities. Misting the enclosure should be avoided unless conditions within the cage have become unsuitable for proper care of ball pythons, as the mother can control the humidity to some degree around her clutch by loosening and tightening her coils. Temperature within the enclosure should remain constant, and if a keeper notices the female making frequent trips to bask, most likely the temperature needs to be adjusted to a slightly higher range. Females with proper conditions for brooding will spend most of their time coiled around their eggs and will leave only to eat or drink. As long as a brooding female's needs are met throughout the incubation period, and the keeper is not insistent upon constant disturbance of the clutch, maternal incubation can be successful. Brooding females, especially young mothers, can become nervous about the safety of her nest if there is too much intrusion by the keeper, and she may abandon her clutch; therefore, it is vital to limit handling and interference except when necessary. Even females that are usually calm and reluctant to bite may become aggressive during brooding, and this may encourage the keeper to keep their distance. Even so, it is recommended that whenever an attempt to maternally incubate is made, an incubator should be available and ready to set up in an emergency should something go awry during maternal brooding.

Typically when a female lays her eggs, they adhere to one another so that they remain together should the female need to leave the nest to feed or drink; however, this is not always the case, and keepers may find themselves with "rolled out" eggs from time to time. Rolled out eggs are those eggs that have not adhered to the rest of the clutch and roll away from the others when the mother leaves the nest. Sometimes these eggs are deliberately rolled out by the mother if she believes them to be infertile, but simple candling can determine the viability of these eggs. Other times, an egg that is not adhered to its clutch mates may accidentally roll out as the mother leaves the nest. If a viable egg is turned out of the clutch, there is no cause for concern as long as the egg has not suffered trauma or gotten dangerously cool or damp. As long as the egg is placed back within the female's coils and is incubated normally with the rest of the clutch, the egg should still develop and produce a healthy hatchling. Most of the time, females will gather up any unintentional roll outs when they return to the nest, but on occasion they do miss them. It is for this reason that while frequent intrusion is discouraged, consistent observation is recommended for brooding females to be certain they are coiling all of the eggs. "Snowflaked" eggs can be a bit tricky to deal with when maternally incubating, as they tend to produce more roll outs since they do not typically adhere to each other as well as normal eggs.

Photo courtesy of Sandy McCoy

A snowflaked egg appears to have spots or snowflakes on the shell, and is believed to be caused by a deficiency in calcium in the mother. Though these eggs may look odd, most are viable and should not be thrown out, especially without candling them. If any particular rolled out egg becomes a problem, the female should be carefully removed, the egg placed back within the clutch, and the female returned to her nest; however, this should be done as quickly and with as little disturbance as possible.

While for many years keepers assumed that brooding females would not accept meals, recent success of maternal incubation has proven otherwise. While many refuse the first offered meal, some will accept subsequent meal offerings that are smaller than their typical meals; smaller meals are easier to digest, and brooding mothers do not need to withdraw too much energy from their clutch in order to consume them. Even if the females do not accept weekly meals while brooding, a ball python refusing food is fairly typical, so it is not a major cause for concern. The female will leave her clutch in order to feed once food is offered, but she will return to brood again upon consumption of the meal. This will not adversely affect the eggs, since in the wild the females may leave the nest for multiple reasons during brooding; in captivity this disturbance is minimal if she is provided with the proper conditions, and her absence while feeding will not disrupt the development of the eggs.

During maternal incubation, duration can range from 50-70 days, and it is important to point out the potential dangers of cutting eggs in a maternally incubated clutch. A cut shell no longer provides protection from a brooding mother that has not yet sensed it is time for the clutch to hatch, and she may accidentally squish the egg to the point of either harming the baby inside or manipulating the yolk in such a way that the baby cannot absorb it. If there is some reason warranted for cutting the eggs, they should be moved to an artificial incubator before doing so. When the eggs are naturally ready, they will begin to wrinkle and finally pip, at which point the mother will loosen her coils in order to allow her hatchlings to leave the nest. However, many babies remain in the egg for a while after pipping in order to finish absorbing the yolk. Once all of the babies have completed this process and left the nest, the mother will then abandon the nest as well.

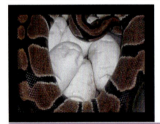

Maternal incubation photos courtesy of Sandy McCoy

Sexing Babies via Cloacal Popping

Sexing neonates is typically done by a method referred to as cloacal popping, but the popularized shortened term of simply "popping" is most often used, and is a method of sexing the baby snakes that involves everting the hemipenes of males. Popping, if done correctly, does not harm the baby snakes in the least. However, one should be aware that any snake going into a shed should not be popped, as this can cause damage to the skin.

To pop a baby, one should place a thumb on the anal scale just above the vent, pulling back slightly to open the cloaca. The thumb of the

Python Passion's Ball Python Encyclopedia

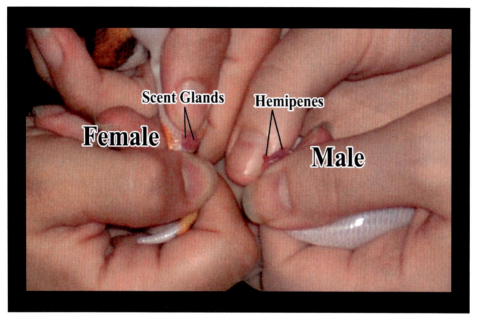

other hand should begin towards the tip of the tail, and be rolled towards the opened vent, similar to squeezing toothpaste out of a tube. A common mistake made during popping is that one often doesn't grasp low enough on the tail with the hand rolling toward the vent and in effect "pinches off" the hemipenes and does not allow them to evert. Most male ball pythons' hemipenes will extend from the vent towards the tail for approximately the length of 9-15 subcaudal (belly) scales. Keep this in mind when popping and try to begin applying pressure past those scales. The hemipenes are little pinkish or reddish rods that pop out, and females will often evert their scent glands in response to the pressure; sometimes distinguishing between the two sexes can be difficult, especially if one of both sexes are not available for comparison.

It is best to sex the neonates before they reach two weeks of age, in which case they gain sufficient muscle control to make the popping method not completely accurate; some males, once they gain sufficient muscle control, may not evert their hemipenes. One can only be 100% certain of sex if they do in fact evert the hemipenes, and any "females" sexed after reaching 2 weeks of age may in fact be males.

Neonates
A full belly of yolk will tide the babies over until after their first shed, typically within 10 days of hatching. Other than checking on the babies daily, it is important that they be left alone for the most part until they begin feeding; it is critical that the babies are able to hide away and feel secure enough to begin feeding. Once the babies have their first shed, it is very important that the babies are checked to make sure they have removed all of the shed skin, especially the eye caps and the tip of the tail, as this can cause problems in the future if left unchecked. After the baby sheds, it should be offered a live pinky rat. Don't panic if the baby refuses food for a few weeks; it takes some babies longer than others to figure it out. It is important to point out here that babies should not be offered food more than once every 5-7 days; on feeding day, place the pinky rat into the baby snake's enclosure and leave it overnight. If the baby refuses its food, simply remove the feeder and wait until the next scheduled feeding day before offering food again. Repeat this process every week until each baby begins to feed. It is suggested that these animals be offered live prey at first, but should be switched over to pre-killed food at the first opportunity.

Feeding Tricks for Picky Eaters
Once the baby reaches 4 weeks old, it should have already begun to feed; should one have some babies that are problem feeders, here are some tips to help those picky eaters begin to feed:
- At 4 weeks of age, place a live hopper mouse in the baby's enclosure. Keep in mind that a hopper mouse can do some damage to a snake if left unsupervised, so be sure to observe the baby and its prey at all times. If the baby has not fed within 30-45 minutes, remove the feeder, as most likely the baby is not interested in feeding. However, most baby ball pythons will begin feeding with this first trick. If they do, offer them another mouse hopper at the next feeding, then attempt to switch them to a rat pink at their third feeding. If they do not feed on the rat pink within a few hours, offer the mouse hopper again. Attempt to switch the baby to

rat pinks each week until they begin feeding on them.
- If the baby reaches 5 weeks of age and is still refusing food, attempt the above trick again. If they still refuse food, remove the feeder and leave them alone for another week.
- At 6 weeks of age, do not attempt to feed the baby. Clean out the cage thoroughly and add additional cover in the cage: this cover can be crumpled newspaper if necessary. The idea is to give them something more to hide behind or underneath. Leave the baby alone for an entire week.
- At 7 weeks old, attempt feeding another mouse hopper.

At 8 weeks old, the baby should already be feeding on its own. If not, place the baby and a pinky mouse in a deli cup lined with a damp paper towel. Make sure to place the deli cup in a warm, dark, low-traffic area. Repeat this process until the baby begins to feed. Keep a close eye on the baby, and make a note of any significant changes, such as a prominent backbone, noticeable weight loss, or loose, hanging skin. Should any of these changes occur and the baby has not yet begun feeding, an attempt at assist-feeding will be required.

Assist-Feeding
Sometimes one will have particularly difficult hatchlings that continue to refuse food. If the baby is noticeably losing significant weight, the baby will need to be assist-fed until it begins feeding on its own. Since this is highly stressful to the snake, it is important to only resort to assist-feeding when absolutely necessary. First, use a small pre-killed or frozen/thawed feeder, such as a rat pink or fuzzy, or smaller if the snake is particularly small, and make sure it is warmed up slightly above room temperature. Then, grasp the snake just behind the head, placing the thumb and first finger on either side of the neck, making sure not to block the esophagus. Stretch out the neck as much as possible, though the baby may be fighting against this. Place the nose of the feeder against the nose of the snake, and gently rock the feeder up and down against the snake's mouth, pushing gently. When the snake opens its mouth, apply very gentle pressure as the feeder is pushed back into the mouth. Try to at least get the head of the feeder into the throat, and

then slowly pull back the hand grasping the head of the snake, and give the snake a moment to relax. Once the snake has gotten comfortable, it will sometimes wrap around the prey at this point, or may simply begin swallowing. In either case, slowly and gently release the snake back into its enclosure, and close them up as gently as possible to avoid disturbing them. Leave them alone for at least fifteen minutes, then check back to make sure the snake has taken the meal. It may take anywhere from two to four assist-feeds before the baby begins feeding by themselves. After two assist-feeds, first offer prey to the baby, and if it refuses, assist-feed again. Continue offering food first each week before assist-feeding, until the baby begins to take food on its own.

Force-Feeding
If after attempting assist-feeding a few times, the baby will still not take a meal, force-feeding will be necessary. When force-feeding, one has two options: the use of a syringe with a baby-food mixture or a pinky pump.

When using the baby food option, the following will be needed:
Syringe*
1½-inch piece of flexible tubing, one end cut at a 45° angle*
3 tsp. chicken baby food, without vegetables
1 tsp. egg
1 tsp. water
½ tsp. reptile calcium powder
*One may also substitute the syringe and flexible tubing with a medicine dropper for pets

To begin, remove the needle from the syringe, and place the flat end of flexible tubing on the end of the syringe. Combine the baby food, egg, water, and reptile calcium powder together and mix until no lumps remain. Fill the syringe with one teaspoon of this mixture, and apply pressure to the plunger until the mixture reaches the end of the flexible tubing. Grasp the snake just behind the head, placing the thumb and first finger on either side of the neck, making sure not to block the esophagus. Insert the angled end of the tube into the snake's mouth until it reaches the throat. Apply slow, gentle pressure to the plunger of the syringe, allowing time for the snake's muscles to swallow. This should be done every three days, since the baby will digest this much faster than a regular prey item, until the baby begins regaining weight. Unused mixture can be stored in the refrigerator for later use, but be sure to allow the mixture to reach at least room temperature if it is needed for subsequent feedings.

The pinky pump option is slightly different, but the idea is still the same. With a pinky pump, one needs to place a thawed, warmed pinky with the tail removed (the tail often jams the grinder) into the end of the pinky pump and screw the end back onto the pump. The pinky pump grinds and purées the pinky before outputting it to the feeding tube. The method of inserting the feeding tube into the snake's throat and using a plunger to push the contents in is as described above. This should be done once every 5-7 days until the baby regains weight and strength.

Once the baby has gained enough grams to fill back out and regain strength, attempt assist-feeding again, progressing to simply offering prey until the baby begins striking and constricting prey on its own.

Selling Babies
If one plans to sell any babies that have been produced, it is recommended that each baby offered for sale has had at least three consecutive, voluntary meals. Any baby that is not feeding or must be assist- or force-fed should not be offered for sale until they begin to consistently feed on their own. The seller will not be viewed in a positive light if the babies being provided are not healthy and feeding voluntarily, and it places the seller's reputation at risk. Some breeders will offer baby snakes at shows that have not yet begun feeding, but if one chooses to do so, make sure the baby is clearly marked as such and is priced accordingly. Also, speak to any potential buyers before the sale and make sure they are aware of the issue. An experienced keeper is the best owner for any baby that is not yet feeding. Most ball python keepers are not easily fooled, and may require pictures and weights of

any offspring they plan to purchase. It is also a good idea to keep track of every aspect of the babies, including sheds, defecations, feedings, and bi-weekly weights charting each baby's growth. Not all potential buyers require this information, but many may prefer it.

Genealogy

While this is not a text on morphs, we will cover the basics of genetics, such as recessive, incomplete dominant (more often referred to as co-dominant), and dominant traits. Understanding genealogy is a complex process, especially in the triple-gene or higher morph animals, but the basics will be covered here.

Genetics for a certain trait are carried on the alleles, a certain section of the DNA that produces skin color or pattern; these alleles are actually mutated from the normal or wild type genes. The alleles are paired, and one is inherited from each parent. The easiest way to determine inheritable traits is by using the Punnett square. The Punnett square is so named for the man who created it, Reginald C. Punnett, and is a simple diagram that allows one to predict the possible outcome of a breeding project. In its simplest form, that of a single-gene animal, it is a grid containing nine boxes arranged three high and three wide. The top center and top right boxes are used to record the traits of one parent, while the left center box and lower left box are used to record the traits of the other parent. Lower-case letters are used to represent a recessive trait, and upper-case letters are used to represent incomplete dominant or dominant traits. Keep in mind, however, that this method of figuring probability of genetics is merely a theory, and nature doesn't always work out exactly as the theory. When using Punnett squares, we are trying to determine *probability* of clutch results, not *actual* clutch results.

For an example, an albino ball python is a homozygous recessive, meaning it has inherited a recessive albino trait from each parent. The visual albino would have traits listed as "aa". A wild type, or normal, ball python has normal traits that are dominant over recessive traits, and would be represented as "NN."

Python Passion's Ball Python Encyclopedia

The Punnett Square, Step 1:
Enter the potential breeders' genetic information into the Punnett square; one parent's traits should be listed in the top center and top right squares, and the other parent's traits should be listed in the left center and bottom left squares. In the example to left, the albino parent is listed at the top, with the recessive albino gene listed as "aa" and the normal parent is listed along the left side, with the dominant normal gene listed as "NN."

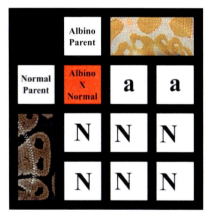

The Punnett Square, Step 2:
The two squares on the left, in this case containing the traits of the normal parent, should be duplicated to all of the boxes to their right. These are the traits the normal parent is passing to all of its offspring; therefore, each of the four boxes would need an "N" placed within it.

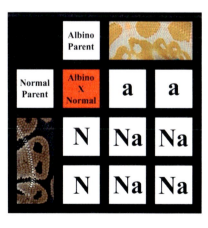

The Punnett Square, Step 3:
Finally, the albino's traits, which are listed along the top, also need to be added to the Punnett square. Each trait here needs to be duplicated to all of the boxes below them. These are the traits the albino parent is passing to all of its offspring. Each of the boxes here list the second trait they have received from their albino parent, in addition to the trait they received from their normal parent. In this case, all of the offspring would be "Na," which means

they have inherited one albino gene and one normal gene; since the normal gene is dominant over the recessive albino gene, their outward appearance is that of a normal, while they carry the gene for albino.

Recessive traits
Simple recessive traits are not visual morphs except in the homozygous form, meaning the animal in question has two genes for the same recessive trait, similar to the inheritance of blue eyes in humans. If an animal has one recessive trait and one dominant or incomplete dominant trait, the animal is considered to be the heterozygous form of the recessive trait, often shortened to "het." For example, a hypomelanistic, or hypo, ball python is a representation of a homozygous snake, and contains two genes for hypo. If breeding a hypo to a normal, the Punnett square would look like the example below:

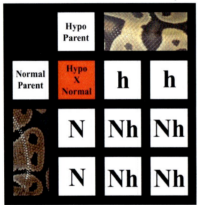

Hypo: hh, Normal: NN, Het Hypo: Nh
All of the resulting offspring are Nh, meaning they carry one normal gene and one hypo gene, and are therefore considered heterozygous, or "het" for hypo; their outward appearance is that of a normal, but they carry the gene for hypo and may pass it along when bred.

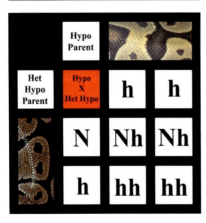

If the heterozygous animal is raised to adulthood and bred to another visual hypo, the resulting Punnett square would look like the example to the left:

Hypo: hh, Normal: NN, Het Hypo: Nh
The resulting offspring in this pairing would be half "Nh" representing heterozygous offspring, and half "hh" representing hypo offspring.

Python Passion's Ball Python Encyclopedia

If the animals to be bred were both heterozygous hypo, the Punnett square would look like this:

Hypo: hh, Normal: NN, Het Hypo: Nh

The offspring in this pairing would be 25% "NN" (normal), 25% "hh" (hypo), and 50% "Nh" (het hypo). When describing the chances of the normal-looking offspring being a heterozygous animal in this case, one must look at the four offspring in question: one of the four is a visual hypo, the other three all look normal, but two of these three will carry the hypo trait, and therefore all three remaining normally-appearing offspring are considered 66% possible het for hypo, until grown, bred, and proven as either het or not het.

If a heterozygous hypo was bred to a normal, the Punnett square would be as follows:

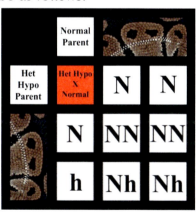

Hypo: hh, Normal: NN, Het Hypo: Nh

The offspring here would be 50% "NN" (normal), and 50% "Nh" (het hypo). However, since all of the offspring retain the look of a normal, the entire clutch is considered to be 50% possible het for hypo until they are grown, bred, and proven out.

Incomplete Dominant traits
Incomplete dominant, or co-dominant, traits are those which are dominant over the normal gene, and will produce a visual morph merely from inheriting a single parent's mutated gene. However, they also produce a "super" form when these same mutated genes are received

from both parents. Typically, the super form is a more pronounced, easier to discern form of the trait. A pastel is a good example of an incomplete dominant trait. A ball python that receives a pastel trait from one parent is a visual pastel themselves, but since this trait is dominant over the normal gene the snake received from the normal parent, this means the animal also carries one normal gene. Keeping in mind that incomplete dominant traits are dominant over normal genes, the normal gene is now represented as a lower-case letter, and the incomplete dominant gene is listed as an upper-case letter, a Punnett square for producing single-gene pastels would look like this:

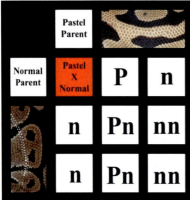

Pn: Pastel, nn: Normal, PP: Super Pastel
In this case, the normal parent will pass normal genes to each baby, and the pastel parent will pass a mutated pastel gene to half of the offspring, resulting in half of the clutch being "Pn" (pastel) and the other half of the clutch inheriting "nn" (normal). Sometimes it is easiest to think of an incomplete dominant gene as inherited in the same manner as recessive genes, but the gene presents itself visually in any offspring that have obtained one gene whereas recessive traits are not visible unless they have received paired genes; in effect, incomplete dominant traits are "visible hets" for the super form. In order to obtain a super form, one

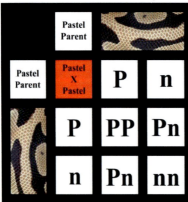

would need two of the same incomplete dominant traits bred together. The Punnett square for creating the super pastel would look like the example at left:

Pn: Pastel, nn: Normal, PP: Super Pastel
Here, the resulting offspring are 25% "nn" (normal), 50% "Pn" (pastel), and 25% "PP" (super pastel). The super pastel is visually much more

discernable from the single-gene pastels.

The super pastel, when bred to a normal, would produce only pastel offspring. A Punnett square for the super pastel bred to a normal would be as shown below:

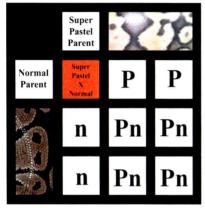

Pn: Pastel, nn: Normal, PP: Super Pastel

The resulting offspring are all "Pn" (pastel) since the super pastel parent only carries pastel mutation genes and can therefore only pass on pastel genes, while the normal parent passes a normal gene to each of the offspring, resulting in single-gene pastels and no normals.

When breeding a super pastel to another pastel, the resulting offspring are half pastel and half super pastel:

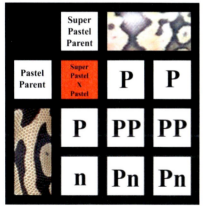

Pn: Pastel, nn: Normal, PP: Super Pastel

The super pastel parent passes on only pastel genes while the pastel parent passes half pastel genes and half normal genes. The resulting offspring are 50% "PP" (super pastel) and 50% "Pn" (pastel).

Dominant traits
Dominant genes are those genes which are dominant over the normal gene, similar to the incomplete dominant genes; however, dominant genes have no visual super form. They are inherited in the same manner as incomplete dominant genes, but those with paired genes for the same dominant trait look no different from those that inherited a

single dominant gene from one parent only. It is easy to differentiate between super incomplete dominant traits and single-gene incomplete dominant traits, whereas it is not in dominant trait animals.

The spider morph is an excellent example of a dominant trait. To produce single-gene spiders, the Punnett square would look like this:

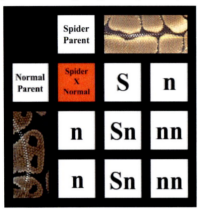

Sn: Spider, SS: "Super" Spider, nn: Normal

Here, once again, the normal parent passes only normal genes to all of the offspring, while the spider parent will pass a spider gene to half of the offspring and a normal gene to the other half of the offspring, resulting in half of the clutch inheriting "nn" (normal), and half of the clutch inheriting "Sn" (spider).

To produce "super" spiders, one would need to breed two spiders together; however, since spider is a dominant gene with no visible super form, a "super" spider visually looks no different than a single-gene spider, and it is impossible to discern between them unless they are bred. The Punnett square for creating the "super" spider would look like the example below.

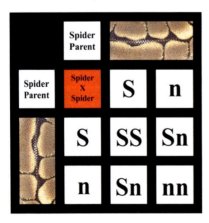

Sn: Spider, SS: "Super" Spider, nn: Normal

The results would be 25% "nn" (normal), 50% "Sn" (spider), and 25% "SS" ("super" spider), however, the "super" spider that received two spider genes would not visually differ from those that only received one spider gene.

The super spider, if it exists, when bred to a normal would produce only spider offspring, since the "super" spider parent only carries spider mutation genes and can therefore only pass on spider genes, while the normal will only pass on normal genes; in effect, the visual differences are not there, but the genetic differences are. However, one has no way of knowing which spider is the super until it is bred and proves out to be.

Combination Morphs
When combining morphs, one must keep in mind that each mutated gene is either dominant, incomplete dominant, or recessive only to the normal gene, not to each other mutated gene, since each different trait is carried on separate sets of alleles within the DNA; even if a snake inherits a recessive trait from each parent, resulting in a visual recessive, they may also receive a dominant or incomplete dominant trait from one of the parents as well, and this would also manifest itself visually in addition to the recessive trait. The exception to this is the case of mojaves, lesser platinums, butters, and other traits within the blue-eyed leucistic complex which are believed to all be carried on the same set of alleles; this is why when any two of these different traits are bred together they produce blue-eyed leucistics just as breeding two of these same traits together does.

Paradoxes
Chimera is an interesting concept that is still relatively new to science. Though it is still being studied, chimera is the most obvious scientific explanation for paradox animals. A chimera is an animal that has inherited two genetically different sets of cells, usually from two separate zygotes or young embryos; the two separate sets of cells merge themselves into one animal but retain their own characteristics. In effect, chimeras contain four sets of parent cells rather than the typical two. It is anyone's guess which organ receives which sets of cells, with perhaps the liver, heart, eyes, and blood receiving one set of cells, and the sperm or ovaries, kidneys, gall bladder, and spleen receiving the other set. This condition is thought to produce eyes of different colors in humans, and is also thought to produce paradox ball

pythons. There can be paradoxes in which both of the inherited sets of traits are for the same morph, such as normal/normal or pastel/pastel paradoxes, though these would most likely never be discovered to be paradoxes unless for some reason the snake was intensely DNA tested. The most obvious paradoxes are those that contain two genetically different morphs within the same animal; these can be anything from normal/albino paradoxes to mojave/blue-eyed leucistic paradoxes. The visual manifestation of both genetic sets of cells often creates a beautiful an entirely unique animal. Most chimeras can breed, though which set of reproductive cells the chi-

An example of a paradox ball python. "Skittles," as she is named by her owner Steve Beamer, is a silver streak (super pastel black pastel) albino piebald paradox.

Photo courtesy of Steve Beamer and Reptile Collective

mera received usually isn't known until bred, and this can be a long process in the case of recessive traits; multiple pairings with a visual morph of one of the chimera's visual genetic characteristics should produce the visual morph at some point if the chimera inherited the morph's reproductive genes, but it will never produce a visual if it inherited the other set of reproductive cells.

Closing
What is perhaps most ironic, snakes are considered to be a primitive form of life since they do not have separate openings for waste removal or reproduction, as do mammals; however, they do have a more

complex sensory organ, the Jacobson's Organ, and two separate openings in which to feed and breathe. While some may think of them as primitive, others may tend to think of snakes as highly developed, especially when in reference to the lifestyle in which they live. Snakes have managed to diversify enough to adapt to conditions in almost every part of the globe, except where it is especially cold, and the earliest snakes have been around since the early Cretaceous period, nearly 100 million years ago; more diversified families of snakes had emerged by the end of the Cretaceous period, around 65 million years ago, beginning their reign on the globe. Snakes now number over 2,950 different species, with more being discovered regularly.

Bibliography

Mattison, Chris, *The New Encyclopedia of Snakes*, Princeton University Press, New Jersey, 2007

Deitsch, Rik J., *Reptiles* Magazine, March 2007, From the Greeks to the FDA

Pavia, Audrey, *Reptiles* Magazine, December 2011, Herp Hideaway

There are many websites in which to research ball pythons; some are credible and some are not. Included in this list are trusted sites which have been directly used to research this publication. Others may have been used as well to a lesser extent, though many websites come and go at an alarming rate, and it would be impossible to list them all.

http://thesnakekeeper.com/index.php?page=bpbasics
The Snake Keeper Ball Python Basics Page - Dan and Colette Sutherland

http://animal.discovery.com/guides/reptiles/snakes/anatomy_03.html
Animal Planet's Reptile Guide

http://www.reptilechannel.com/kid-corner/beyond-beginners/snake%20anatomy.aspx
ReptileChannel.com's Snake Anatomy Page

http://www.reptilechannel.com/kid-corner/beyond-beginners/snake-anatomy-respiratory.aspx
ReptileChannel.com's Snake Anatomy Respiratory Page

http://www.reptilechannel.com/kid-corner/beyond-beginners/snake-anatomy-cardiovascular.aspx
ReptileChannel.com's Snake Anatomy Cardiovascular Page

http://www.reptilechannel.com/kid-corner/beyond-beginners/snake-anatomy-gastrointestinal.aspx
ReptileChannel.com's Snake Anatomy Gastrointestinal Page

http://www.reptilechannel.com/kid-corner/beyond-beginners/snake-anatomy-immune.aspx
ReptileChannel.com's Snake Anatomy Immune System Page

http://www.leedspetshops.co.uk/index.php?main_page=page&id=69
Nutritional Value of Prey Items for Snakes

http://vpi.com/publications/determining_the_sex_of_snakes
Vida Preciosa International - Determining the Sex of Snakes, Dave and Tracy Barker

http://ballpython.ca/gallery/breeding.html
Markus Jayne Ball Pythons Breeding Page, Mark & Jayne Mandic

http://thesnakekeeper.com/index.php?page=bpbasics
The Snake Keeper Ball Python Basics Page, Dan and Colette Sutherland

http://www.rcreptiles.com/articles/why-do-female-ball-pythons-python-regius-coil-so-tightly-around-their-eggs.pdf - RC Reptiles Article on Maternal Incubation Study

Made in the USA
Columbia, SC
13 December 2018